THE BOOK OF DONUTS

THE BOOK OF DONUTS

poems

edited by

Jason Lee Brown & Shanie Latham

Terrapin Books

Terrapin Books
4 Midvale Avenue
West Caldwell, NJ 07006

www.terrapinbooks.com

ISBN: 978-0-9982159-4-5
LCCN: 2017950413

First Edition

For those who bake them,
those who consume them,
and those who write about them

Contents

Between the optimist and the pessimist, the difference is droll.
The optimist sees the doughnut; the pessimist the hole!
—Oscar Wilde

I owe it all to little chocolate donuts.
—John Belushi

Introduction

You can't buy happiness, but you can buy donuts.
And that's kind of the same thing.
　　—Anonymous

Every country claims this sticky, fried piece of dough as its own, but historians, in their supreme fiction, insist that the Dutch were the originators of doughnuts. Oily little lumps, *Olykoeks* were identified in the nineteenth century as holiday specialties.

But imagination met legend when shipmaster Hansen Gregory stuck them on his ship's wheel spokes to have better use of his hands. That legend sounds weird unless we do more wiki digging and find it was his mother who filled the center with nuts and packed them off with Hansen to take aboard in 1847. It seems plausible that this captain may not have liked nuts and nutmeg (and maybe not even his mother). Why would he have wasted the centers? And how, then, did he steer? Or manage to eat them?

Let's move from fantasy to facts.

There are dozens of explanations for the doughnut's shape and significance, but we know for certain that this sweet thing took a coherent path to the future, becoming an American icon, in the early part of the twentieth century when a doughnut machine was invented in New York City. We all know that American ingenuity and industrialism are indispensable to the integrity of mass production (plus sugar and fat). From that moment, the doughnut, with its basic beauty and inner honesty, would serve a new and larger purpose at every imaginable event—from CEO conventions to Jiffy Lube waiting rooms, as a centerpiece for political party causes, human stories in rehab, police coffee breaks, and so on.

Surely doughnuts have been in our landscape from our first babysitter's bribe, yet it took poets to bring aesthetic insight to every aspect of the doughnut's contribution to society. Poets couldn't wait to get their little computer-stained fingers on them. Even though otherwise engaged on Mount Olympus, they came down for a moment to share a commitment to this fried dough that has been with us through the Charleston dance, War Bonds, the Studebaker, Laurel and Hardy, General Eisenhower, the Cultural Revolution, and rock 'n' roll to now—needed, as never before, to balance our Nike-biking-pilates-obsessed-low-cal-coffee-latte lives.

Editors Jason Lee Brown and Shanie Latham selected fifty-four poems by fifty-one poets, happily including Denise Duhamel, Jack Bedell, Mira Rosenthal, Martha Silano, Julian Stannard, Charles Harper Webb, among others. With all poets singing together, we have a rainbow of words—alive, nourishing, rich—that clearly define the range and power of the once humble doughnut. Poetry and confection make for a delicious marriage. And who knew we'd live to see sugar, fat, and dough connected to the divine?

In "Donuts, the Color Of" Jim Daniels describes, exceedingly well, the noble cause a substantive doughnut plays in his work life: "The air smells // like—cold dirt? Factory oil smell / on my hands. Inside, I am careful not to touch the glass / counter while I point at the fat donuts // with thick white cream inside, the ones that are bad / for you, the worst." The speaker says, "I inhale the warm dough and coffee. I sit / on a round red stool. /... / The roads are lined with black-whiskered snow. / How about that? Snow that smells like exhaust. / Exhaustion. Every morning I pass the yellow donut lights— / how can I explain—I'm drawn to the lights ..."

Katrin Talbot's "Punctuated by Donut" is a true narrative able to articulate, with affection, the doughnut as an archetypal relief, one of the many evolving messages, in this book, that a sweet fried lump is an emotional calculus for comfort: "But every drive home from / the MRIs, CAT scans ... / we'd stop by / the kosher donut shop ... / and sink our teeth in / the temporary cure for / everything."

And what of singing a child to sleep with "Blacktop Donuts, a Lullaby"? With motor engines as her background, Anne Harding Woodworth changes the mood from danger to comfort with the thought of a simple halo of dough: "I closed the window / and laid you down out of my cuddle. // You cried a protest without conviction, / as if you knew that tranquility was to be // yours in things male and rough."

In "Donut Shop" David Hernandez reconciles a philosophical rumination: "My reasoning has more holes // than a colander as I wobble across the iceberg / of life's meaning, clueless as the next guy // who happens to be stepping out of the donut shop / carrying a dozen. Wish I had one. Glazed // or chocolate. One that dusts my lips and powders / the floor like snow shaken off a crow's wings."

Charlotte Mandel, in "Sufganiyot for Hannukah," writes about the jelly doughnut as a mechanism of religious service and remembrance, an aspirational thing, while Richard Newman, in "Donut Tree," writes about doughnuts as a marriage of values, magnifying the strength of another culture—Majuro, Republic of the Marshall Islands. He says, "... and now my turn / in line, I know, not seeing any bags / but only smelling moist, delicious air //... that they've sold out / again ..." His speaker later says, "Crossing the coral rubble ocean side, / we stand on crumbling graves emptied by waves / and squint into the wind, the blurred horizon, / a ukulele above the rising tide."

Elizabeth O'Brien describes the consequences of living in the wrong city but being able to get some relief: "The heft of the bakery // door opening; / donuts and hot coffee. / Across the street the lit-up / marquee of the grocery, / open 24. The blue air / almost thawing."

And so, fifty-one poets with fifty-one points of view come together, in complicity, each writing their own true thoughts about a sticky, sugary bun. This confection, molded and fried, often enriched with raisins, chocolate, cream, or jam, is a single unity of pleasure where we can have our cake and eat it too—if we buy a baker's dozen.

Poetry, like the doughnut, begins with a sticky mass which we shape into consistency, compress, then form, making our own small cakes of conviviality and gratification. After you read this book, try your hand at combining disparate elements into your own wondrous creation, and then why not write a wondrous poem about it.

Doughnuts (Basic Recipe)

3 ½ cups sifted all-purpose flour
4 ½ tsp. baking powder
½ tsp. mace
½ tsp. nutmeg
½ tsp. cinnamon
1 tsp. salt

3 T. shortening
1 cup granulated sugar
2 eggs, well-beaten
1 cup milk

½ cup minced nuts (optional)
approx ½ cup sifted all-purpose flour

Sift together first six ingredients. Work shortening with spoon until creamy. Add sugar gradually, continually working until light. Add eggs, beat well with spoon. Add flour mixture alternately with milk, blending well with spoon after each addition. Add nuts and enough of the ½ cup flour to make a soft dough. Chill one hour or longer.

Roll dough on floured board to ½" thickness, cut out with floured doughnut cutter. Form extra dough into a ball; roll and cut as before. Fry in 1½" oil to 370 degrees F. When they rise to surface, turn with long-handled fork (do not pierce). Turn often until golden and done. Drain on paper, cool, and serve as is, or dust with powdered sugar, or shake in a paper bag containing sugar.

—Grace Cavalieri

Grace Cavalieri produces and hosts "The Poet and the Poem" from the Library of Congress for public radio. The author of nineteen books and chapbooks of poetry, she is also the author of two cookbooks: *The Poet's Cookbook: Recipes from Tuscany;* and *The Poet's Cookbook: Recipes from Germany.* Her awards include the 2013 George Garrett Award, the Pen-Fiction Award, the Allen Ginsberg Poetry Award, The Corporation for Public Broadcasting Silver Medal, and the inaugural Columbia Merit Award for "significant contributions to poetry."

What Shaped You

At eleven, you already knew
some things didn't last—
a father's careless love, a marriage,
holes best filled by home and summer,
perched in a dripping bikini
on a stool at the counter of Britt's Donut Shop,
doors flung open to tourists' laughter
and the carousel's calliope,
as you dove into the sugary bliss
of glazed grease hot from the fryer,
gobbled before ocean air turned it soggy.

What you didn't know
was that even homes don't last,
that your mother would move you
without warning two hundred miles inland
to a cavernous house, a disquieting
stepfather who served boxed Krispy Kremes:
bready, not melt-in-your-mouth
light and airy. Warmed in the oven
till they filled the rooms with a scent
familiar but not quite right,
not carried on a breeze flavored
with popcorn, seaweed, cotton candy.

—Pam Baggett

Beignets

I want to show my daughter
how much her grandmother
loved making beignet dough.

Such simple work:
metal bowl, warm water,
yeast and sugar,

eggs, milk, and salt.
A quick whisk, and cups
of sifted flour.

My daughter's hands,
shaped so much like Mother's,
would be perfect for kneading,

for making smooth this dough
as sticky as any memory.

—*Jack Bedell*

Most Bizarre Beauty Queens of the 1950's

—after an article by Elyse Wanshel

It's easy to snicker at the Sausage Queen,
draped in a stole of glistening, tumescent weenies,
a quintet of bratwurst bristling from her pasteboard crown.
Or 1954's Miss National Catfish Queen, posed with a monster
catch and one supple leg proffered, like the reenactment
of some lesser-known Greek myth. And what happened
to the blueberries that filled the Hotel Roosevelt's tub
in which the Blueberry Queen slithered? Did someone
make the World's Largest and Most Unhygienic Cobbler?
But something makes me return to the photo of Joy
Harman, New York City's 1957 Donut Queen.
Perhaps it's the impossibly unanatomical upthrust
of her sweatered breasts, cantilevered to the ceiling.
Or the hint of teeth and tongue between her lips,
making me think *bite bite bite.* Or how she's shot
from below, as if the photographer were kneeling to receive
the communion of the small powdered donut she proffers
between her thumb and forefinger. But it's probably
those disembodied hands holding the grotesque
donut crown poised over her head—less of a pastry
homage and more of an oversized lamé ouroboros—hairy
and veined, a signet grinning from the ring finger
that I almost hear saying *this way honey just like that honey
that's great honey a little more honey turn a little*

more to the right honey try not to breathe honey
just one more honey. And Joy later, at home: *No Ma,*
it's not a halo, it was never a halo, not a halo at all.

—*Nicky Beer*

The Third Doughnut

One friend's fight against fever manifested
itself in night-long dreams in which she did
nothing but stack sandbags. When my son
was recovering from brain surgery, he drew
intricate knots of pipes and tubing which looked
like nothing so much as synapses blooming,
stretching to connect. I wonder at the less

obvious ways the subconscious may be
working out my salvation. What else could account
for the time I blurted out to a lovely
lady who asked only to sit next to me
on an otherwise empty bus, "Sorry,
but I don't have any money." Or my decision,
in the bubble-market euphoria before
the Great Recession, to pull my money
from Lehman Brothers and throw it
in a kitchen drawer. But it's not good to think

about it too much, to start second-guessing
one's psyche, to worry that the six dark months
I find myself mired in every year are meant
to help me acclimate to the longer night ahead,
not to mention—and this is pure conjecture—
couldn't one justify that third doughnut

as a prudent laying-in against the coming
famine, the pastry-less apocalypse my lizard
brain has already detected
with its prescient, flickering tongue?

—C. Wade Bentley

Before I Had Been Wise

I should not have had that doughnut, third
in a series—this one avant-garde, maple-
frosted with bits of bacon. Come to think of it,
I should not have had most of the doughnuts
I have had in my life, I'm sure you would agree.
Nor should I have started my walk to the lake
without something to keep off the rain,

the rain I know comes nearly every afternoon,
this high in the mountains. Certainly
I should not have watched so long and with such
morbid interest while the red-tailed hawk
snatched ducklings by the tail as they fed,
upended. And later, as I stripped off my soaked
sweater and muddy boots and started a pot

of coffee on the stove, I should not
have checked my phone messages to hear
that Brenda Lang had died of breast cancer,
that same Brenda who, in the eighth grade,
wrote on my locker in permanent marker
that I should not make the mistake of falling
in love with her. And of course I know

that by the time I realized I had been staring
for who knows how long out the window,
in only my underwear, I should not have lifted

my eyes to the pantry shelf where a raspberry-
filled bismarck, one drop of jam oozing
blood-red in the evening sun, filled my heart,
though I always know it shouldn't, with desire.

—*C. Wade Bentley*

Choux à la crème

I.

I was never alone. I had the comfort
of donuts—sugared, powdered,

glazed—and pastries: mille-feuille,
kouign amann. My favorite?

Choux à la crème. Is it surprising
no one would sit with me in the cafeteria?

There was no confusion
about my role. I was the example

of what could go wrong
if one lacked the will to diet.

Shameful, my classmates' eyes
decried as they skirted past

to join their friends—
slim as egrets.

I told myself creamy delights
were better than friendships.

Even if my life wasn't destined
to be filled as sweetly

as my lovely classmates',
there would always be crullers

and confections waiting
at the end of my day,

not to mention macarons
or chocolate eclairs.

    II.
Years later I avoid bakeries
the way I once slipped past

accusing mirrors.
Whoever thought someone

would call after me
Hey, Beautiful!

To this day I turn to see the stranger
they're hailing,

the thought of being without blemishes
or ratty hair, of being *pretty,*

is at times as foreign as New York
once seemed to be, teetering

on the world's edge. Slowly,
I'm adjusting.

Yet how could I have predicted
that one day my opinions

would be sought? That jobs
would open for me like books

begging to be read? That others
would want to be me?

It's crazy. Inside I'm the same fatty
longing for donuts I was at fifteen.

I'm not that model you imagine, stepping
out of a Pre-Raphaelite painting,

yards and yards of auburn hair
draping down my petite waist.

—*Bob Bradshaw*

Drop Donuts at the Start of Summer Vacation

For there was the yellow kitchen
late on a June morning, Mom stirring milk
into flour in a chipped china bowl. For

there was a pot of hot oil on the back burner,
ready for spoonfuls of fluffy batter that sizzled
as they browned and formed a luscious crust.

For there was a metal mesh basket dripping fat
as it was lifted from the pot, and a plate
lined with a paper towel to drain the newly

fried orbs. For there was a brown lunch sack
filled with powdered sugar, and into it went
the cooled donuts to be jostled until coated

in ivory sweetness. For there was a cut-glass bowl
with faceted blossoms, mounded high, waiting
to be carried into the living room.

For there was Andy Griffith on the TV, and
Dick Van Dyke, glasses of milk and Mom's coffee.
For there was the afternoon ahead, many afternoons

to fill with bike rides, swimming, long walks to the park,
and lazy do-nothing lounging; all the delights
of summer bursting into bloom

with drop donuts as the bounteous seeds.

—*Nancy Susanna Breen*

Elegy for the Last Donut

Pity the poor donut no one took
to avoid being the greedy pig
who grabbed the last one.
It languishes in its cardboard box
on the conference room table, gazing
hopefully through the cellophane lid
as the minutes tick away to quitting time.
If glazed, its glinting veil of sugared ice
melts into unappealing sweat.
If cream-filled, its delectable fluff
turns to spackle inside a wad of quilt batting.
If frosted, the coating hardens, then flakes
like whitewash from the walls of an aged shed.
Jelly remains jelly, but trapped
in a resisting disk of Styrofoam.
Someone might sneak a fragment,
the remainder lying like a dismembered limb
among a littering of colored sprinkles.
Even the cleaning crew can't be enticed
by a cinnamon twist completely undone,
denuded of sugar and spice,
its doughy litheness stiffened with age.

—Nancy Susanna Breen

Xander Gets the Doughnuts

While Buffy slays vampires and saves high school
from another Tuesday night snakeboy apocalypse,

Xander gets the doughnuts.
We all hate Buffy and Willow and Giles

when they tell Xander how lucky he is
to be soft. Creamy centered. He never tells them

doughnuts ended in sex with Faith, with him saving everyone
from the Zombie Bros' basement bomb.

He knows how hormones stuff bodies
with black magic and sweets

until the world crisps and glistens,
lingers between terror and surrender.

Missed curfews and cigarettes lead to vampires.
Jellies and bear claws lead to sex and bombs.

The gang lovingly condescends about his happiness
hinging on a lack of danger, but Xander just smiles,

exits screen right. He's a teenage boy.
He still has time to lick the sugar from his fingers.

—Sara Burge

Guilty Anticipation

I told a student if he came to class late again
he should bring me a cruller.

Except for my husband, I hadn't told anyone yet
that I was pregnant, not even my mother.

I was forty and I didn't want to think what that
might mean. My mother had reassured me

that if Nadia Comănici could have a child at forty
then so could I. And indeed, I did.

That day the student arrived late again.
I wasn't feeling well so I had cancelled class.

The student went to the secretary and gave her
the donut in a brown bag to bring to me.

When I felt better and returned to my office,
I stopped by my desk and ate the donut:

it smelled like the sugar of anticipation;
it looked like the gluttony of guilt.

I devoured it, then prayed for my baby
and my fluttering heart.

—Lucia Cherciu

Doughnut Ghazal

How easily our happiness bloomed—*doughnuts*
the word Father said. "She's gone. Let's make doughnuts."

She was off giving birth, May '65, to redheaded Michael.
Father assembled ingredients for deep-frying doughnuts.

As the army trained him, he cleaned the kitchen first.
He had the cookbook open: beignets, crullers, doughnuts.

Two eggs, sugar in a sparkling mound, one cup
of milk. He had a secret touch for making doughnuts.

How little we knew of supper night after night, meal
plan, vitamins, casserole. Our taste was for doughnuts.

Another time it was rock salt and ice, making peach ice cream.
Happy to turn the crank. Fun, like deep-frying doughnuts.

O when she returned, it was asparagus, lima beans, peas.
Patricia wanted another kid—let Father make doughnuts.

—Patricia Clark

Lent

In this season where sugar turns ash,
                Mama and I rise before school
      to buy fasnachts, buttery lumps
                  of potato flour, from the best bakery in town.

I wear chapstick to trap sugar on my lips,
                to hide between my teeth this metaphor
      for everything I'll lose in Lent,
                this promise: what I love can leave me.

I know no matter how many prayers I hurl
                into heaven, I can't take back the kiss seared
      on Jesus' brow, the bread of his bones.
                I can't save Mama from mourning,

and so, as always, her love will wither like a bulb
                buried too close to winter, vanish like hallelujahs
      from our mouths. No praise now, because Lent
                is the wrong season for joy.

I know better than to test her, but I do it
                anyway, holler *hallelujah* when the sky spits snow,
      wide flakes that'll turn to rain that night.
                She grinds her teeth and doesn't speak to me

until dinner: *Jesus,* she prays, *make us sorry*
                for our sins, offer us the grace to repent.

We sing hymns until long after bedtime—
        let all mortal flesh keep silent,

ponder nothing earthly-minded—
        and I'm almost sorry.
    But the next day, soot-cross darkening my forehead,
        I bless everything on the playground:

worms scooped from the sidewalk return alive
        to the soaked earth, *hallelujah,*
    only two girls murmur *freak* and point at me,
        hallelujah, when a ball whistles from a boy's hand

it misses me, *hallelujah,*
        my teacher lets me stay inside for the rest of recess
    and I fill the empty chalkboard, the tail
        of each *a* like the tongue of a lily:

hallelujah, hallelujah, hallelujah.
        These blessings, not for me, not for them,
    but for Mama: as if blessing something
        is the same as fixing it.

As if enough forbidden praise
        could drag Jesus back before he leaves us,
    leaves her alone and wanting what I can never
        give her, some love other than mine.

     —Emily Rose Cole

Rationalization

Fry, dunk, sugar, cajole, bathe in cinnamon, sprinkle
cha-cha dancers on smooth whiteness,
ice like Jackson Pollack. Thank the Dutch

for every *olykoek*, palm-size, four hundred calories
wide, one hundred calories deep.
Isn't calorie a measure of heat? Ah, sweet crutch:

chocolate glazed, cream-based, two-a-day. Straight
from mouth to hip. Can you swallow it?
Food hit of the century in 1934, way too much

for tubbies. Loosen up. *Krispy Kreme* rhymes
with dream. Go ahead. Wallow
in a carrot-cake donut, call it a vegetable.

—*Betsey Cullen*

Donuts, the Color Of

After midnight shift I drive down Mound Road
long straight pot-holed
magnetic ribbon connecting factories and shops.

The sky is the color of—well, it's going from black
to blue in a way that makes the yellow neon
of the donut shop seem warmer. The air smells

like—cold dirt? Factory oil smell
on my hands. Inside, I am careful not to touch the glass
counter while I point at the fat donuts

with thick white cream inside, the ones that are bad
for you, the worst. I feel like a dirty rag ready
to be thrown out. I might spontaneously combust.

I inhale the warm dough and coffee. I sit
on a round red stool. People nod to each other
in this Church of Day Just Begun and Day Just Ending.

Nothing to talk about.
The roads are lined with black-whiskered snow.
How about that? Snow that smells like exhaust.

Exhaustion. Every morning I pass the yellow donut lights—
how can I explain—I'm drawn to the lights like—
I know these cream-filled bombers

aren't going to save me, but they're antidote enough
to take home to bed, the weight in my gut a solid thing.
Yellow, white. The colors of angels.

—*Jim Daniels*

In Praise of Donut Sellers

Lard smooth and slightly warm,
the donuts' glaze cools quickly
to a fine, pale crust, fragile
as a dust of snow. You're up north,
working your way through grad school,
slinging decadent Boston creams, fleshy
jelly-filleds, heavenly French twists.
You've gained more than a few pounds—
damned leftovers. Sometimes, you
heave them into the trash, vulgar balls
of sugar and fat. Other times, you
box them up for shelters. More
often than not, you bear them home
like treasure. After several months,
you realize how deeply you hate
the flippin' donuts, the bakery, that
fecund, yeasty smell, the thick caul
of grease and powdered sweetness
melded to your skin. You detest
the white apron, the plastic gloves, the scale,
the flies trapped and buzzing
in every shiny case. Today, at the end
of the after-church rush, you watch
the woman beside you who is so much
older, her hands worn, her blonde hair
dyed and brittle, the one whose bad grammar

decorates the air. She's toiled here
for years. You try to make small talk:
She has a condition. Her husband
skipped town. She's dating
the deli guy who slips her
fantastic cuts of beef. She wants
more than anything to buy her daughter
a double-wide home. Before you
can stop yourself, the words flop
out of your mouth: "I can't wait
to get a real job." Silence. Silence. A glare
thick as dough. You want to suck the syllables
back between your teeth, swallow them
down into darkness. "This is
a real job," she says, voice a flinty shard,
and turns her crooked back. Flames
rage in your cheeks. The jig
is up—she knows what you are
as you stare at the sticky floor, as you stand,
dizzy and naked, beside the lemon custards.

—*Heather Lynne Davis*

The 1000th Barrel

Boiling and frying Dough Nuts.
      —Logbook, 4/8/1843, *Charles W. Morgan*

Dough-drunk and jovial,
some whalers even sing and jig on deck,
while others carve teeth and bone,
one reads. It's like an extra
dogwatch, but instead we celebrate
the occasion of so much oil
casked and stowed, and all are cordial:
captain, mates, whalemen,
even men disgruntled
with their lot share a grin
with me, for today I'm not
called *idler,* a cook up to my elbows
in flour, egg, and pearlash,
with a little cinnamon ground
from the captain's own reserve
mixed in, some crumbs
bubbling in the humid tryworks.
That barrel snug down in the hold,
filled so soon on this voyage,
is surely a good omen, our luck
as greasy as the faces slick
with oil left over from this recent catch,
and I tell those eager 'round the galley

as I knead and sugar this last batch:
for certain, boys, before New Bedford is frosted
with snow our rudder will turn toward home.

—*Joanie DiMartino*

Note: It was tradition among whaling vessels to celebrate the stowing of the 1000th barrel with donuts fried in whale oil. Contrary to the hopes of the crew, the *Charles W. Morgan* remained at sea two more years, ending her first voyage in 1845.

First Breakfast in Weihai

I haven't yet learned
how to say hello, *ni hao*, or even
thank you, *xie xie ni*, so I point
to a dish of green sprouts with rice noodle threads,
a bamboo basket of dumplings,
hoping they are filled
with shrimp or pork. I choose
a square pastry stuffed with what
I expect to be spiced cabbage
but bite into sweetness,
like a donut I realize, delighted
to recognize syrupy fruit. And then,

as I glance toward the avenue, a man
hauls three hard-shell suitcases from his taxi
and one plastic bag squared with four flat boxes,
Krispy Kreme the first English words
I've seen today. He lifts the bag
delicately, so pleased that he has brought his family
such an exotic sweet.

—*Lynn Domina*

Mr. Donut

They tumble from closing bars into here.
Uninspired men nicknamed for their hair:
Whitie, Red, the bald one, Flesh.

What a way to save to go to Europe.
But that's what I'm doing,
the donut waitress taking advantage
of drunks. I look through
the fatty blurred window,
remind them often of my aspirations,
drum on the countertop: I am not like them.

Red's got a novelty passport
and motions me over. He thinks
his finger's alluring as Cape Cod,
the farthest I bet he's ever gone.
"Guess where I've been?"
he slurs and has me open the blue book.
A rubber jack-in-the-box penis pops out.

I think of adding sugar to the diabetics' coffee
when they laugh, describing their naked wives.
Twenty-four hours, any day, they know here they can.
There's not even a lock on the Mr. Donut door.
So when there's a fight on the corner, Flesh tells me
to call the police from the phone in back:
"If the bikers see you finking, they'll get your ass."

From behind the muffin case, the motorcycle clash
looks like a home movie: skipping loops, a volume lapse
as bikes are kicked over, heads smashed.
The blood puddles slowly, graying.
Connie strolls in, her lipstick all crazy:
the fight's over her. She wants a light.
I know she'll stain the rim of her cup.

But they all leave big bills under the saucers
and I get to read the few
quiet hours before dawn.

—Denise Duhamel

Portrait

My grandfather left my grandmother with two small children.
Just left, disappeared, never returned.
I'm sure he had his story, but this is mine
and all I know.

My grandmother was a quiet woman
with fine, thin, hair that she could comb to below her waist
       then braid and wind around her head.
A deserving crown.

To allow a man to see her bare feet would not be proper.
She washed her hair in rainwater.
She loved God and Will Rogers.

She made handstitched quilts with the remnants
       of her homemade cotton housedresses.
She made dinner from jars of carrots, tomatoes, corn and peas
       that lined the farm cellar shelves.
She snapped beans straight from her garden
       into the hammock of her hand-sewn apron and
       made milk warm for kittens in the smokehouse.

And she made donuts,

with yeast and flour, butter, sugar, nutmeg.
And eggs lifted fresh from beneath the hen.
She mixed and measured and melted, beat

and let rise to double the size.
And then she cut and fried,
> tossed them in a paper bag of sugar.

My grandmother didn't make a man leave her.
He did that alone.
He alone turned his back on everything warm she once held.
Everything she raised in his absence.

—Jane Ebihara

Ede Market Day

Jetlagged but game,
we bike from your house in Ede
to a busy open-air market where
farmers sell vegetables and cheese—
Edam, Kanterkass, Leyden—
mongers exchanging wedges of Gouda
for exquisite toy money.
Everything is unreal and wonderful:
this is not our world, we have
no stake, no responsibilities,
and I feel as open and dreamy
as the first green day of spring.
A hurdy-gurdy plays, and children
boogie and fall down and get up.
We walk slowly, we try to take it all in,
we want to buy the whole world
and eat it for lunch. Then we find
the true draw, a stout man
with a stainless wonder:
an Oliebollen machine.
He wiggles a funnel
across a lake of boiling oil,
jiggling a switch to release globes
of smooth elastic dough,
plopping them into a smelting
proof to form crisp delicate mounds.

The contraption jerks with each drop;
oil spatters; his hands are
pocked with red marks,
the tattoos of his trade.
Standing in a fugue, I track
the Oliebollen as fluttering gears
lift them from the oil to drain,
and the man dusts them with a ploof of sugar,
a galaxy expanding and settling,
and I feel the gut-tug of love, real love—
falling-in-love love, for that machine,
for the sweet smell of the Oliebollen,
for the friends who brought us
to this perfect moment,
for the market and the town of Ede
and the country of Holland
and the whole world contained exactly
in the round perfect pastry.

—*Sara Eddy*

Epistle to the Donut Shop

Dear Warren Avenue, dear aluminum green awning
beneath which people waiting for the Dearborn bus
dodged the rain: Polish women in dripping babushkas
clutching shopping bags from Fairlane Mall, young black men
headed for the suburbs to look for work, Lebanese
millwrights going home from a grueling shift at Rouge,
dear Golden Boy Donuts, I write to you as I would write
to my parents if letters were still necessary, and they are,
of course, just as every outmoded medium gives us
so much we do not know we need. Dear father
seated in a booth behind a wall of windows, drinking coffee,
reading student essays pulled from an ink-scarred manila folder,
glancing out at the avenue guttering with puddles
and discarded shopping bags while I ate glazed cake donut
holes and listened to Helen and Elizabeth, immigrant
first cousins who owned the place, speak to each other
in Polish (my childhood is narrated by West Detroit
languages I still don't understand except in cadence
and intent, my mother speaking Spanish with Maria Chavez,
our next door neighbor, for hours while the neighborhood
kids ran in the spume of an uncapped hydrant in July;
Shadia Shamsedean calling her children in in Arabic
as the street lights buzzed on). I watched the water runnel
off of you and splay like feathers. Once I tripped in a mud puddle
in the alley, and Helen fished me out and bathed me
in the prep kitchen where they kneaded and cut the dough
and sifted powdered sugar over the Euclidian shapes of pastries,

swaddling me in warm dish towels while we waited
for my clothes to dry. My mother worked midnights in triage
at Receiving, and she slept during the day,
which meant that while we were eating donuts, she was dreaming
of gunshot victims and the stunned doughy faces of cardiac
arrest, of stab wounds like sequined dime purses, near overdoses
with glassy eyes and pustuled forearm scabs, police badges
glinting in halogen light, which meant that while
my father read bad prose written by the 18-year-old
children of auto workers for Composition I at Wayne State
University, my mother's dreams were narrated by a tinny voice
reciting injuries and traumas into an analogue telephone
receiver over a crackling PA. Dear donut shop,
you are gone, not gone exactly, but your lime-green façade
has been painted pink and your smell of dough and coffee
has been replaced by garlic and kibbie, and the Iraqi family
that owns this place came here fleeing a war the way
Helen and Elizabeth came here fleeing war in a wholly
different world, yet a world defined by those twin forces
of violence and refuge, and I love this place still as I love
my mother and father while remembering donut holes
and steaming Styrofoam cups of coffee. Dear Hamido Restaurant,
dear Golden Boy, dear father, dear mother traumatized by all
that you have seen, dear Dearborn, I eat kafta in the same
squat building, watching the blacktop avenue blear with rain
and oil, women in hijabs pushing little wire carts out
of Arab markets, abjad liturgical script above the English
signage, and I'm nostalgic for what hasn't really changed.

—Cal Freeman

The Center

Donuts simmer one by one as my daughter pokes them with
a long wooden spike from the drawer where we keep
skewers for kabobs that my husband grills with pita
whenever we have company; the donuts turn golden in the
oil, bubbling in even circles that gather near the dough, and
she asks if I think they are done, but I am not sure if the
center will be wet dough or if the golden color indicates a
fluffy cake inside and do not know what the outside
indicates about the status of the inside, just as I don't know
what the gages in my daughter's ears (now an inch in
diameter) mean about what she thinks of herself or how it
must feel to have a pierced septum with the black metal
arrows pointing down to her lips (the bottom lip pierced
with snake bites) that don't tell me what she is thinking, but
I see my daughter and her beautiful self that she keeps
poking around to find, piercing each part to find what
matters and where the pain might yield a piece of her that
she could keep beside her bed and have it remind her that
the inside is soft and light and also golden.

—*Anne Graue*

The Sting of the Jellyfish

In my daughter's drawings, we resemble
a trio of jellyfish: our pumpkin-round heads
without torsos, our long inky legs
squiggling playfully down the page
before culminating in feet like oversized breadloaves.

If we are indeed jellyfish, then we're clearly
happy jellyfish, with our upturned mouths,
despite our eyes, which are empty, oblong,
strangely akin in shape to gourds,
potatoes, and yellow squash.

These are the figures that cover
page upon page in my writing notebooks,
that appear like trademarked logos
in the corners of my wife's grocery lists.
Sometimes they even add a dash
of unintended variety to our comments
on students papers.

And they are there too, at night,
taped to every surface I pass
as I make my habitual visit to the refrigerator,
a lonely search party of one,
intent upon rescuing the evening's leftovers
from a long life of isolation and mold.

Three happy, healthy jellyfish, one of us
a bit wider and rounder, a bit top-heavy,
even for a jellyfish, but all of us smiling—
no, beaming, really, and when I look at them,
I understand this is the way my little daughter
believes it will always go for her family.

Sometimes that in itself is enough
so that I return the pork chop
to its cold nest of rice, applesauce, and peas,
re-snap the red Rubbermaid lid into place,
and sneak back to bed with the burn
deep in my belly.

But sometimes nothing is enough.
Not even the memory of walking
into the kitchen at first light,
way back when I was seven or eight,
a scrapyard scattering of assorted donuts
surrounding my mother, who lay face down,
asleep again at the table—this a long time
before the heart attacks or the hospital visits.

I'd whisper her awake, and she'd spring upright,
embarrassed, cruller crumbs and Krispy Kreme
smeared from her chin to the small space
between her nose and her upper lip.
Ask her what she was doing and she'd swear
she didn't know, and I'll be damned
if that wasn't the truth of it.

The devil liked to grab hold of that woman,
and once he turned loose of her,
she couldn't remember a thing.

—*Justin Hamm*

Valentine's Day at the Spousal Loss Support Group

One by one, they straggle in, some bringing
heart-shaped boxes of candy to give the rest,
others with simple Valentines bearing heartfelt
notes of thanks to the group for mutual support.

And then she enters, a bit late, a box of
gooey donuts in her hand, their garish icing
gleaming through the cellophane box lid—
more than enough for all.

Widowed now for two years, she's brought
a variety—some iced with sticky chocolate,
some neon pink, and some glazed vanilla topped
with multi-colored sprinkles.

She's sorry she was late, but she stopped
to pick them up on her way because it's
Valentine's Day, her husband was a cop, and
they always had donuts down at the station.

We pass the box around, carefully lift out our
choices, placing them on the red napkins
she's also thought to bring. We always go out
to lunch after meetings, and many of us

shouldn't be eating this much sugar, or don't
really like such rich and gooey treats, but we
eat them together while sharing our memories,
tempering the bitter with the sweet.

—*Penny Harter*

Donut Shop

The oversized pink donut fashioned on the roof
reminds me of the hole in the ozone dilating

above Antarctica, above the clueless penguins
wobbling over blue ice. Gets me thinking about

rings and holes in general, a life preserver tossed
from a yacht into the frothing waters where

someone's head once bobbed. About inner tubes
and nooses. About halos, glowing like white neon

over the heads of angels swarming around
a benevolent being. Benevolent and powerless

or else another day for the man consumed by waves
to sip a martini on deck. Or else merciful hands

to stitch closed the ozone's wound. Ergo,
God's a hole in the sky, big as the O in Oblivion.

To get from *I don't believe* to *I believe,* one must
jump through many hoops garlanded with flames.

Or one hoop, unlit and inches off the ground.
I don't know. My reasoning has more holes

than a colander as I wobble across the iceberg
of life's meaning, clueless as the next guy

who happens to be stepping out of the donut shop
carrying a dozen. Wish I had one. Glazed

or chocolate. One that dusts my lips and powders
the floor like snow shaken off a crow's wings.

—David Hernandez

Why I Cried Reading This at Liss and James' Wedding

—not just because I was pregnant
but because the last line was hers

Some people fall in love just around the edges. For others
love is fireworks in fog, true grandeur unrecognized,

password never guessed, beautiful torture missed.
For Melissa, James, it's immersion, discovery, engagement.

The sign outside the psychic's read *Today Only, Readings $10.*
But the sign was not painted to use just one day. Today Only

is a lucky charm. Time, peaceful as tap water, begins now,
poured into one glass to sustain you, today, another day

and more. You'll be kind to one another, and he'll bring
laughter home. You'll build the peace of the home, she

will amaze you with wit. She is voluptuous and volatile,
he is anchor and oxygen, diving under together, bravely,

to see a freshly-washed-window view of the full world.
Today only is that fine moment when you finally hit the jelly

in the donut's center, and stand together shining in that wide,
united way a diamond throws light, a carpenter builds a deck

and a view, a pond in the back, with a waterfall. May you be
a perfectly ripe pear, "yielding to gentle pressure," a sure sign

of readiness. And carry on, gently, and then you will find
a carriage ride, a sweet old Ford pickup, a hammock, a sea.

—*Tina Kelley*

The Light on Everything

Near the tent the parents glide about their business, the sisters giggle and hiss over who sleeps where, and the snakes are all quiet at once. It is not as dark as it seems out here. Imagine the perch glinting deep in the pond and the cow path starry. The father draws the honey buns and Wagner's orange drink from the cooler veiled by flame and scrolls of smoke. He gathers the family to the aluminum lawn chairs settled in the red dirt. A breeze exhales a breath of sagebrush across the water. Peeling back the cellophane bit by bit, the adults eat from one end of their honey buns to the other. The children discard their wrappers and proceed, following an unspoken rule as sacred as a proverb, as important to their lives as rock-paper-scissors and wishbones.

> do not bite across coils
> rather follow each ring
> along its unwinding

—Kim Lozano

Free Samples Field Trip

Campfire Girls in the seventies,
we craved not log and flames,

tent and bags, not even beads
sewn neatly in rows across

the felt vests decorating our flat chests, but
crullers, fritters, long johns, Boston creams

clicking, I-Love-Lucy style,
on too-quick conveyer belts

past our seventh-grade hunger
as we sat off to one side,

mesmerized behind display glass,
on turquoise counter stools.

It was the best-tasting show in town
and so technological:

pumps and pistons, dunk
and sizzle, the allure

of polished stainless
mixing miracles from the same

boring ingredients our mothers used
for treats with less pizazz.

Monthly, we sang a song of Krispy Kreme,
swore an oath to sprinkles,

stared, and drooled,
and stared again, forgetting,

forever it seemed,
the great sugarless outdoors,

while waiting, somewhat impatiently,
for one magnificently doughy,

end-of-tour, powder-topped,
surprise-filled O.

                    —*Marjorie Maddox*

Sufganiyot for Hannukah

Holiday foods unite spirit with body—
for Hannukah, sufganiyot—
round jelly doughnuts dusted
with powdered sugar. Fried in oil,
the treat recalls ancient miracle—

how a sacred flame with but one day's pour of oil
shone radiant seven days more until
newly purified oil of olive,
fragrant with myrrh and cinnamon,
could be brought across the desert.

On Israeli streets
kiosks spring up fast as dandelions.
Faces of children and their parents
jelly-streaked, lips sugar-layered.
Sparrows pouncing on crumbs.

So delicious to so many
that the Minister of Health
warns of overeating,
and even an Orthodox rabbi
writes in a daily paper, "No need
to fatten our children."

At sundown
parents kindle menorah candles.

Orange-gold flames reflect in children's eyes
as sufganiyot appear on their plates
eight successive days.

—Charlotte Mandel

Afterwards

On the worst days, as I'm about to consume in secret
an entire assorted dozen while seated in my darkened kitchen,
armed with knife and fork, white handkerchief
noosed around my throat, an attempt, I guess, to give
the gluttony a touch of class, I think of each long john as a life
raft, the ringed others as lifesavers tossed into a sea
in which, after breaking half a dozen promises
and eyeing a half-dozen more, I've begun to drown,
not in the oily translucence lingering along the surface
of the box, but in knowing, once again, the delight
I found in the first surrender will be, with each subsequent bite,
a diminishing love, leaving me filled but unfulfilled.
I promise next time I'll buy only one, but know in my heart
that everything about donuts is a lie, that the best part
is their missing center, their resemblance to the me
I've become. When there's nothing left to sink
my shame into, I close my eyes, listen to my teeth sing,
lick the tip of my finger, and, in gentle jabs, search
the crumby tabletop for stray sprinkles, each hoping to be
found, eaten by a lonely someone who shares the pain of existing
on the glazed layer of someone else's idea of perfection.

—Faisal Mohyuddin

Donuts

Last night as temperatures spiraled
toward zero and winds swirled
snow, my thoughts circled back
a few years to a night in Minneapolis
when I did donuts with my little son.

It was January, in an empty
parking lot covered with snow.
In our old black Volvo I turned
to my son and said, "Are you
buckled in? Here we go!"

Under cones of yellow-orange light,
I turned the wheel and hit the gas.
We slid blurry circles across the night-
orange snow, laughing and yelling,
"Whoa! Whoa! Whoa!"

Sometimes you want to give it a whirl,
put all the chips on red—or be a big zero,
a no-show when 8 a.m. rolls
around for work or school. The world
is always turning. I put my foot down

and turned the wheel hard—
a dozen loose and useless circles in the dark.

—*Matthew Murrey*

Donut Tree

—Majuro, Republic of the Marshall Islands

At most a ukulele, a basketball,
maybe a flip-flop above the rising tide,
we queue on sand this morning at Donut Tree
for coffee, vodka, SPAM sushi, and yes,
donuts, while poverty sprawls on either side
like a sleeping dog,

and when not sleeping, the mongrels of Majuro,
gnawed by hunger and mange, would rather chase
a running pair of knees than sun-warmed bowl
of dogfood, have grown too many, too aggressive—
my friends and students, all attacked, some bitten,
as was my sweet mutt Ginger—so any dog
without a collar will be rounded up,
throats slit like pigs, feeding the Majuro
police force and their families for weeks.

Ginger and I walked down to City Hall,
a mostly open-air building, to buy
a tag to fasten to her collar, five bucks.
The clerk behind the counter had no change
for a $20. "Can you come back tomorrow?" she asked.
At least I now had time for the Donut Tree
before my weekly student lit mag meeting

which always helps attendance as the students
magically seem to know when I have donuts.

In any other place, these donuts—hard,
unglazed, unsprinkled in brown paper bags
Rorschached with grease stains—might be tossed for rats,
but here on Majuro, they take the shape
of our atoll, where the hole is our lagoon,
the glorious blue center of this life,
and everything around it is moist bonus,
and if I take two bags to Liberal Arts,
they will be gone in minutes, and Jae, our small
Korean Marxist geographer, will eat
a whole bag on his own, and now, my turn
in line, I know, not seeing any bags
but only smelling moist, delicious air

of deep-fat sugar-dough, that they've sold out,
again, the last bag left
the counter hours ago, and this has happened
four of the last five times that I've stopped by
the Donut Tree, and I am once again
left with the hole, the fragrant nothingness
implied by donut, and this is why these donuts
are so delicious—because they're sweet and rare,
because the Donut Tree's a lottery
we only savor if we're lucky, because
sometimes in this sad but carefree place,
only emptiness feeds our emptiness.

Crossing the coral rubble ocean side,
we stand on crumbling graves emptied by waves
and squint into the wind, the blurred horizon,
a ukulele above the rising tide.

—*Richard Newman*

Donut Day at Inglis House

Fridays the wheelchairs roll in
steered by hand, head, and tongue
in more variety than the donuts they seek
after a week of healthy food.
Coffee is held to the lips and sipped
or drunk through straws,
thickened to the consistency of sap.
Donuts cut into bites
and forked into mouths,
the pot tilted until the last drop is gone
and chairs power up.
Each donut-eater heads for the door
carrying off bits of the morning—
jelly, chocolate, sugar, glazed—
every face etched with its own flavor.

—*Michael Northen*

How the City Percolates at Dawn

I could almost live
anywhere in the bluegray
liminal hours of morning:
pushing coffee and extra donuts
on everyone, *take one more*
on the house, please. Minneapolis,

you are brown, beige, and almost
new. Neon, granaries, sheepskin.
Bridges and nothing but.
Even the invisible reservations
everything in you silently rests on
seem to shimmer, almost

molt. Hennepin and 24 is haloed
by Lite-Brite x point bulbs. Once
on a bus, I saw a shirt that said, "Minnesota
is for punk-ass bitches."
The shirt was blue. The bus was passing
the Walker.

Tolerance is the policy
here. The state flag is a tattoo
in the shape of Minnesota
and everyone's tattooed. How people—
not me—love it here. It's moving, somehow,
as if you are the greatest city, which you aren't;

you're just Minneapolis, where I'm living
for now, my latest attempt
to attempt
whatever it was. But in Boston,
where in my heart is home, love
means not to leave. And here I am—

goddamn Minneapolis—a waypoint
between newlywed and wherever
I'm going next. What else is new. At this hour
you're still in bed;
the mellow hum of empty buses.
The heft of the bakery

door opening:
donuts and hot coffee.
Across the street the lit-up
marquee of the grocery,
open 24. The blue air
almost thawing.

—*Elizabeth O'Brien*

Sugar Dust

Winter powders rooftops, lawns,
pink Daphne buds closed like tiny fists.

In Cheyenne once or maybe Rawlins,
cold blasted my cheeks, bit fingers and lips,

followed us to the car where we huddled,
my brother and sister and I, hurled

from Wyoming, chocolate milk cartons
and doughnuts in our laps, windows lacy white,

Mother and Father counting cash, inching
miles on a map that wouldn't add up.

This isn't sugar dust or glazed nostalgia. What I recall
is the pinch of early spring, harsh light, the howl.

—*Keli Osborn*

The Days of Donuts

We used to get wasted and take the van out to spin
across the lake, the party-on-wheels a drama depending
on who was dating who or how impossible our futures.

I took my wife to a Dunkin' Donuts to explain the allure
of pastries she didn't know from growing up in Sao Paulo,
each bear claw and fritter a stale reflection of childhood.

The particle accelerator experiment could open a tiny black
hole, the negation of all matter the true mission of humanity
on the days I read the news, which lately has been often.

The snow never let up in the years we skidded into craters
and our own future shadows, addictive powder and dizziness.
My wife wanted to try donut holes and I passionately refused

to embrace change, confused by how tastes and times tatter.
The experiments of mashing atoms is not unlike bodies
tumbling in a van or raw dough sizzling into a stellar glaze.

The tempest of taking chances spins me at times into motion.
No man my age should put something like that in his mouth.
The end of the world is a dot in the distance pulling us along.

—*Martin Ott*

Donut Hole

Everything has a hole
in it: borders with openings, lists
with omissions, loves with transgressions, an
awkward silence in the hive of an angry diatribe.
Tears are repaired. Dig a hole and someone has to fill it.
My aunt couldn't sing. My uncle could. Drive away and you
have to find your way back again. Gain requires loss. It's quite

elemental. Theories have   undeveloped parts that
require the breathlessness   of unequivocal data. No
place is special, different   from any other. No mo-
ment of time is different   from any other. *Such a*
messy world isn't it dar-   ling, said Wallis Simp-
son to her Duke. Even   with bluebells on the
far hillsides, there's mud   on a servant's shoes,
the fat man must sit still   in his seat not to disturb

the others, while the worm keeps burrowing in the earth his
observable truth: a hole. A past that can be revisited is
not passed. Emptiness is a there. Einstein sitting at
the counter of some furnace of calculation,
an amplification of $1+1=2$. Thinking:
I'll have some sprinkles on that,
not the plain one.

—Brent Pallas

5 World Trade Center

Home in Indonesia we watched by night
plane after plane crash into the towers and the towers
come crashing down and I thought in the crash
of recollections in the hours that followed
of the sweet servers at a Krispy Kreme beneath
the Plaza we visited every year at least once
on our trips to my New York hometown.
The company declared the store destroyed
though workers and customers escaped
unharmed and pictures surfaced later
showing trays of donuts waiting still to be told
where to go while a rag and spray bottle
of cleaning solution lay on a table under
a profound film of dust no one wiped away.

—*James Penha*

Connecting Dots and Donuts

Solution for a bad-hair day: the donut-do. Twist and twist
into round bun and pin to head. Worn by the white, English-only
teachers who forbade Spanish in their classrooms—smacked us
with wooden rulers when we whispered in our only tongue.

> Every country has its doughnut: round or flat—filled,
> dipped, or braided. Greece has *loukoumas*. India has
> *balushahi* and *gulgula*.

When I was little, we'd fry dough balls in sizzling lard,
the soft O's floating up a golden brown. Sprinkled
with powdered sugar or cinnamon. I preferred *buñuelos*:
tasty fried tortillas—like Mamá's *canela abrazos*.

> Peru has *cachanga* (like *buñuelos*). Chile has *sopaipas*.

Mamá usually wore her hair pinned up in a messy bun, to keep
it from her sweaty face in endless housework, and toiling in the
crop fields with Papá or our whole family. She gained weight
easily, tried to stay away from snacks and our homemade donuts.

> Italy has *ciamballe, krapfen, zippuli, bombolone*.
> The Netherlands has *oliebollen* (literally "oil balls").

My mother spoke little English but understood much. She wore no
makeup. I was ashamed of her overweight and plain appearance.
In old photos, she looks prettier and thinner than I thought!

Norway has *smultring*. Spain has *berlinesas*.

My hair-up days are over. Prefer it down, shoulder length,
a hair band or sun visor to keep it from falling on my face.
My granddaughter Julia likes to wear her hair in a
pretty bun or ponytail, both "in" these days.

Finland has *munkki.*
Morroco has *sfenj:* often soaked in honey.

Julia and I have a tight bond. Facetime, texting, emojis connect
us when we can't visit. She took Spanish in middle school,
learned to string lines together—ancestral seeds replanted.

South Asia and Middle East have *Jalebi.*
France has *beignets*, meaning "bump."

The extra sugary donuts from Krispy Kreme and Dunkin' Donuts
sweeten sad memories. I eat one, maybe two—excess
causes a different pain.

Mexico has *sopapillas, churros, pan dulce* (sweet bread).

Mami passed away two years before Julia's birth. They would
have loved each other. Often my memories twist like a tight
bun, feel vacant like a donut hole. I jam my days with sweetness
and healing to undo old knots, fill the hollow of the sour years.

—*Anjela Villarreal Ratliff*

Six Visions of the Donut

1.

Give me a sidewalk-crack fizzing with ants.
A donut dropped on the hill-mouth disappears
as the colony swallows it whole.
Shouldn't each ant explode on contact?
No, they carry many times their own weight
in sweetness. Ants have the talent
to hold raptures that big, a pink that brazen,
to take more than they've ever needed and make a haven.
If there is a god, they can taste what they carry.
When the queen receives the offering
with St. Theresa's ecstasies,
do her eggs fill with sparks?

2.

Give me a donut-heavy trash bag
slung by anarchists. Let it drop
to the college coffeehouse floor.
We are just honey-starved strangers
until we watch dumpster divers
and bandana-tied varmints squatting
to pluck crullers from the black bag.
We raise our heads to stagger
toward them and touch hands
over the open-bag glow.
Praise the teenage late-night clerks

who bag the days' donuts
without dumping coffee grounds over them,
praise dumpster covers waiting
like prayer hands for opening,
praise anarchy and sugar riots.
Where are we without
a hole to fall in all night?

3.

Give me a cool white plate,
your sharpest knife, and a Krispy Kreme.
The teacher's lounge stretches
a dozen to almost a hundred.
The teachers twitter waistlines
and balance a delicate eighth
between their fingers—orchid-weight
and sugar-shattered, each bite
is just right until it's over. Each swallow
is a sweet, retracted offer.
The plate is cluttered
with the crushed dome of heaven.
How many have you had?
No one is counting.

4.

Give me the round around
the nothing to see here and the sound
of sugar grinding in a regular's teeth.
Give me the lost and found bin at the topless
coffee shop in Vassalboro, Maine,

where the cast off T-shirts read:
I donut give a damn.
Donut talk to me. Donut forget
to smile. Donut judge me.
Donut mess with Texas.
The city muscles the coffee shop down
until even $6 refills stop paying the bills.
The pastor says, *I hope it's replaced by a more*
family-friendly establishment.
The regulars regret the loss of regular glories:
stories, hallelujahs, nipples, donuts.
Dear God, what is more
family-friendly than that?

   5.

Give me the slow lines of Oregon
outside the donut shop. Give me
the spiral-bent people weave.
Rain lasers on sparkling bricks and the wish
on wish on wish for a coffin full of black-glazed,
donut voodoo. Who do you think you are,
hanging your nose on the hook-sweet scent
of whiskey sprinkles and pretzel pins?
Listen to the sprint in your veins
as you walk in a slow, rained-out parade.
The blazing floats are inside
behind lit glass rotating spells in the ether.
Help me. I'm hexed-out and lost,
my brain bashed with hankering

and visions of sugar bombs. Wait,
I know you. We shared at donut once.
Will you marry me?

    6.

Give me the counter.
Give me the wait. Give me
the warm grease-bag weight.
Give me the crave-eyes.
Give me the Eucharist with sprinkles.
Give me a last supper.
Give me the bent-wing,
blissed-out brain-haze of muses.
Give me high-fructose bruises.
Give me cute and useless.
Give me fluke inventions sliced thin.
Give me a slick of sin on cake.
Give me now what I won't take.
Make it mine.

       —*Meg Reynolds*

Job Offer in Mobile

Years from now, when we live on the Gulf
in Alabama—why not?—we'll raise our two kids

high in the air so they can see the fantastical
Mardi Gras floats go by, hundreds and hundreds

of plastic beads flung to the sky. Later, we'll cull
the best, then take the rest of our rainbow pyramid

to Dunkin' Donuts to trade for a more practical
dozen of plain glazed, those little wicked

sinkers we eat, even if they make us sluggish
come noon. And we won't need to keep being true

Americans who pick up on a whim, as they say,
and go fishing for what's better in another metropolis.

This moving from place to place makes me blue.
So take another sip of coffee, and let's stay.

—*Mira Rosenthal*

Pączki at Easter

Her turkey was dry, the kind of parched that dreamed
in feathers: flight worthy by sight, too heavy to soar,
and meals were simple—meat, potato, milk,
cucumbers for a vegetable, scored
with fork tines, sliced into daisies, pretty
but tasteless, and if dinners weren't her bag,
the *pączki*, well, the *pączki*, were what we lived for,
the fattening before the fast, all four
of us lined up to fill the paper bags
with clouds, cooled and sifted-sugar pretty,
like snow on mountain tops, we thought, and scores
all stuffed with plummy jam to down with coffee milk
because, lifted from the want of Lent, we soared
before we lived the kind of parched that dreamed.

—*Marybeth Rua-Larsen*

How Scientists Get Made, or How is a doughnut like a coffee cup?

Somewhere along the way
you will have to learn about
calculus, physics, black holes,

but it starts with the ordinary,
a white paper plate
cut in a spiral,
string tied to one end,
a rock glued in its center,
with which you explain
to your classmates
how air moves.

You get hooked
at the science fair,
vow to win,
make papier-mâché
volcanos, watch them blow,
harness electricity
in a glass jar, grow
blue-green mold
on a slice of Wonder bread.

At this stage,
it's not science you love,
but the mess
you can make: stuff

gurgling, scorched,
the stench
of rotting matter.

Your mom reads
Jules Verne to you
nightly, hoping
to fire your neurons,
dad buys you a telescope
and a chemistry set;
they read up on Einstein
and MIT, plan vacations
around planetariums.

Along the way,
you realize
what's only existed
in your head
can be made
real, can explain what
you didn't understand,
or teach you how
to ask a question.

Soon you progress
to the novel,
an exploding piñata,
a talking Chia pet,
and the profound—
walking on water.

This is you
by the fifth grade,
the surprise that
this is also you at twenty,
thirty, forty—your skill
for grant writing—
sophisticated begging,
your ever-patient mother calls it
—matched by a desire
for the perfect experiment
and a willingness to fail.

Your scientist friends
make ludicrous bets
(porn subscriptions and
gentleman's wagers)
on how flat, cool,
doomed the planet is,
how small the particle,
how large the universe,
but for you it's the beauty
of a question that beckons:
how is a doughnut like a coffee cup?

—*Anne Sandor*

Note: Davis Thouless, Duncan Haldane, and Michael Kosterlitz
won the 2016 Nobel Prize in physics with the answer to this
question.

What can I say that hasn't been said

about the old-fashioned glazed, the buttermilk bar,
the feather boa, the maple blazer blunt? Truth is,

I eat them rarely, less than once a year. I hadn't
considered my ascetic life till I sat opposite

a woman smiling and moaning as she licked
each spoonful of tiramisu. What's become

of the kid who ate so much Rocky Road
she made herself sick? I want to be that girl,

oblivious of the connection between indulgence
and a thigh's girth, between powder-sugared lips

and the needle on a scale, but I am so far gone,
so not a sensualist as I jog past Voodoo Donut

where the bearded and the tattooed, the pierced
and the ski-capped, wait for their Dirty Snowballs,

their Tangfastics, their Raspberry Romeos.
I'm overdue for a Pot Hole, a Diablos Rex,

to down an entire bag of Sprinkle Cakes,
my mouth transformed to an icing rainbow.

Where is that me who raced to the front door
when her uncle showed up with the box

of Dunkin' Donuts, eager to devour the goopiest
jelly, the most velvety Bavarian Kreme?

—*Martha Silano*

Donut

Oh, Benjamin P. Lovell, 19,
from Oneonta, New York State,
who appears in the Police Blotter
in Thursday's *Daily Star* for
unlawful possession of marijuana.
The Police Blotter hangs just
below the cast of *Hairpsray*
rehearsing at the SUNY ONEONTA
GOODRICH THEATER
where the girl playing Tracy
Turnblad looks as if she's been
helping herself to donuts:
maybe the donuts we were eating
at Barlow's General Store, Treadwell.
Do you ever get an upstate rush?
I've never been crazy about donuts
but these are the aristocrats
of the donut world and I salute them.

And I hope, Benjamin, your mom
isn't going to be too mad as she casts
her eye down the Police Blotter
and sees your name there, *You little shit!*
and I hope the authorities remember
being young when the whole world
sometimes seemed somehow like
a gargantuan donut that either pulled

you to its bosom (O Tracy!) or kicked
down—somewhere—to the bloodstream.
Sweet donut, do I love thee? I haven't
mentioned Brando K. Goodluck, 18,
from Manhattan, charged with seventh-degree
criminal possession of a controlled
substance. O Brando, O Brando,
what were you thinking?

As I put a donut in my mouth,
I'm thinking I wouldn't mind
a joint, and, in any case, maybe
all these donuts are pretty dangerous
and I wonder what would happen
if the rules got jumbled up
and the girl playing Tracy Turnblad
slid down the page
and found herself in the Police Blotter
charged with unlawful possession
of a donut. Suddenly America feels
different and I like it. Police
Blotters throughout the nation
packed with donut-heads and half the country
on the run as college girls make
secret calls and meet their dealers
in dusty ghost towns, sweet
vapors drifting through the trees.

O America, where even the robins
are bigger, where every car that

slides into the forecourt of Barlow's
General Store is a Dodge, where
half the population is chasing
the perfect donut. Let's imagine
that Benjamin P. Lovell and
Brando K. Goodluck, nice slim boys,
who've never touched a donut
in their lives, wander into Barlow's
and roll a joint and talk about those
losers who kneel down before "the big one."
They know the girl who was playing
Tracy Turnblad. She was sweet, they say,
who went and threw it all away
for a sleazy bun with a hole in it.
They pass the joint to me and I can
feel the donuts I stuffed in haste
somewhere down my slacks. I blush.
You boys want more coffee?
The donuts on her shelves have gone.

—*Julian Stannard*

Small Bites

As a girl I ate a donut in small bites
to make its sweetness

last, its sugar coating
a mother's softness

I couldn't remember,
a promise of love.

I hid powdered sugar donuts
in the back of a kitchen cabinet

to savor when the grown-ups
were gone,

when I ate
as if loneliness could end.

—*Carole Stone*

A Doughnut and the Great Beauty of the World

I try not eating the chocolate one with sprinkles
and I don't succeed—my pledge to my diet dies,

but the taste validates my backsliding, the fine
smudge on my lips beautiful as lipstick on a woman.

Someone wrote "the great beauty of the world"—
maybe I did, I can't be sure—and I believe the words.

I remember the ugly of the past and I know the worst
of the future is already gearing up to make its visit—

I finish the doughnut, clean away the evidence,
and head back to the couch to finish a book I love.

—*Tim Suermondt*

In the Key of Donut

Have you ever tasted a donut
in a minor key?
Heard a solo cello
sing an elegy for a
sister's fritter?
A glazed requiem?

The display case with its rows of
tiny little hallelujahs,
the smiling clerk's C Major
What would you like?

And we all walk out,
our white bags or boxes
carrying non-liturgical,
cream-filled doxologies for our
little lives of powdered sugared
praise.

—Katrin Talbot

Punctuated by Donut

The only thing sweet about
those months before
the diagnosis was
the girl, *my* girl,
as she soldiered through
the medical tests,
the chronic head pain,
the almost unbearable
fatigue.

But every drive home from
the MRIs, CAT scans,
the doctor's blind
fishing trips,
we'd stop by
the kosher donut shop—
our luscious comma'd routine—
and sink our teeth into
the temporary cure for
everything.

—Katrin Talbot

A Highly Caloric Lament

A pox upon you, Charlie's Chili Dogs,
Dunkin' Donuts, Coldstone Creamery,
you harpies of the dreaded calorie—
quit hitting on me till my judgment fogs,
and every vein and capillary clogs
with drippings from your latest recipe!
Arugula? Not for the likes of me,
and neither are those dreadful diet blogs.
Been there, done that—gave all my sweets away,
ate naked salad, kept the flab at bay.
But nowadays my magnitude increases.
I'm getting tubby. Fatter by the day.
Just look at me: mine aft has gang agley,
my life's in shreds, my mind's in Reese's Pieces.

—*Marilyn L. Taylor*

If Only

If only the caress
of the finest cashmere,
the slide of silk on skin,
or buttery leather
on cold, cold fingers
could erase the absence
of a lover's warm hand
on the small of the back.

If only the sweetness
of a well-frosted donut,
chilled buttercream roses,
or the darkest chocolate
on those trembling lips
could compensate for the loss
of the tart taste of love
on the tip of the tongue.

—*Eileen Van Hook*

Babci's Apron

Pączki make me punchy,
send me yearning
for my grandmother's
kitchen in Brooklyn,
the aroma, the taste,
the joy of eating
jelly donuts
as fast as
they were made
with no thought
to calories,
no concerns
about fats.
She'd just fry them up.
We'd just eat them up,
then wipe our sticky hands
on Babci's apron,
imprinting our handprints
to memory alongside
Dziadek's prized
red rose bush
on the fire escape
where, when full,
we sat with Grandpa
in the sun.

—*Dianalee Velie*

I Am Not a Jelly Doughnut

But President John F. Kennedy—
he of the Bay of Pigs and Camelot—may
have claimed to be one when he said,
"*Ich bin ein Berliner,*" a Berliner being a kind

of jelly doughnut for which Berlin is famed.
That little *ein* filled JFK with cherry goop
and plopped him down in scrambled eggs.
Still, his meaning was clear: "I can't enjoy

democracy's jelly doughnut unless others
have one, too." He felt that way about Marilyn
(who called him "my little jellykins").
He couldn't enjoy her unless brother Bob did, too.

Representative Anthony Weiner couldn't
enjoy his namesake organ all alone. That's why
he e-mailed pictures to young women,
precipitating Weinergate and turning the jelly

doughnut of his future into a cow pie.
How bravely he had borne his name—
refusing to blush when kids called him
Weinerhead or teachers pronounced it

(out of politeness) *Whiner.* "No, ma'am,
it's weiner, like the hot dog," he replied.

Running for class president, he won
with "Elect Weiner-man," "Climb into

the Weiner's Circle," "Vote for a Proven
Weiner," which he *was* until one wrong
keystroke exposed his hot dog to the world
and proved again that names *can* hurt,

as when I asked for a Berliner at Sol's Deli,
and a white-haired man with numbers
on his wrist leapt up and mashed a jelly
doughnut in my hair.

—*Charles Harper Webb*

Blacktop Donuts, a Lullaby

I stood at the open window
with you in my arms, bathed, fragrant,

soft, and ησυχος, as your Greek grandmother
would say of you—because you were tranquil.

In the empty church parking lot
across the street, a Firebird and a Mustang

pulled in fast. Brakes skidded across
the gravelly surface. Engines growled,

revved in place, as lights shot out
into our darkened neighborhood,

until the cars split from one another
and began to pivot on front tires,

while the rears swung into circles
and tail lights stream-blurred. Rubber

heated into smoke, gravel arced like sparks
pinging against metal. And you stirred

in my arms, as whoops of risk and danger
penetrated the quiet of your sleeping place.

Boys whirled cars dervish-like, loud
and howling in ecstasy. Their arms hung down,

their arms pumped as open orbs, signs
of violent emptiness, appeared in the grit

of the blacktop. I closed the window
and laid you down out of my cuddle.

You cried a protest without conviction,
as if you knew that tranquility was to be

yours in things male and rough.

—*Anne Harding Woodworth*

Contributors

Pam Baggett's work has appeared in *Crab Orchard Review, Nimrod,* and *San Pedro River Review.* She hosts poetry readings, teaches writing workshops, and is a recipient of the 2017 Ella Pratt Fountain Emerging Artists Grant from the Durham, North Carolina Arts Council. She has never found a better donut than Britt's, which still thrives.

Jack Bedell is the author of several poetry collections, most recently *Revenant.* He is the recipient of the Louisiana Endowment for the Humanities Individual Achievement in the Humanities Award and the Governor's Award for Artistic Achievement. A Professor of English and coordinator of the creative writing programs at Southeastern Louisiana University, he also edits *Louisiana Literature* and directs Louisiana Literature Press.

Nicky Beer is the author of *The Octopus Game* and *The Diminishing House*, both winners of the Colorado Book Award for Poetry. She's received awards from the NEA and the Poetry Foundation, and her work has appeared in *The New Yorker, The Nation, Best American Poetry*, and elsewhere. An associate professor at CU Denver, she edits poetry for *Copper Nickel*. She was raised on Long Island Dunkin' Donuts.

C. Wade Bentley teaches and writes in Utah. A chapbook of his poems, *Askew*, was published by Red Ochre Press in 2013, and a full-length collection, *What Is Mine*, by Aldrich Press in 2015. He has published poems in such journals as *Best New Poets, Rattle*, and *Poetry Northwest*. Donuts are his spirit animal, his patronus, his constant companion.

Bob Bradshaw is a retired programmer living in California. His poems are included in both volumes of *The Crafty Poet: A Portable Workshop* and have been published in such journals as *Apple Valley Review, Eclectica*, and *Pedestal Magazine*. His work has also been featured in *Autumn Sky Poetry Daily*.

Nancy Susanna Breen has published three chapbooks of poetry, including *Rites and Observances* (Finishing Line Press) and *How Time Got Away* (Pudding House Publications). She edited nine editions of *Poet's Market* for Writer's Digest Books. She believes in the power of donuts to stoke the poetic muse.

Sara Burge is the author of *Apocalypse Ranch* (C & R Press). Her poetry has appeared in *Prairie Schooner, Virginia Quarterly Review, River Styx,* and elsewhere. She teaches creative writing in Missouri and enjoys raspberry-filled doughnuts as often as possible.

Lucia Cherciu writes in both English and Romanian. She is the author of five books, most recently *Train Ride to Bucharest* (Sheep Meadow, 2017). Her work has been published in such journals as *Antioch Review, Connecticut Review,* and *Tinderbox.* She is a Professor of English at Dutchess Community College in Poughkeepsie, NY.

Patricia Clark is the author of five volumes of poetry, most recently *The Canopy* (Terrapin Books, 2017). Her poems have appeared in *Prairie Schooner, Michigan Quarterly Review, Salamander,* and elsewhere. She was poet laureate of Grand Rapids from 2005-2007 and is Poet-in-Residence as well as a Professor in the Department of Writing at Grand Valley State University in Michigan.

Emily Rose Cole has received awards from *Jabberwock Review, Ruminate Magazine,* and the Academy of American Poets, and her poetry has appeared in *Nimrod, Spoon River Poetry Review, The Pinch,* and elsewhere. She is a writer and lyricist from Pennsylvania and is a PhD student at the University of Cincinnati.

Betsey Cullen studies and teaches poetry at the University of Delaware's Osher Lifelong Learning Institute. Her work is included in the anthologies *Prize Poems, 2017* (Pennsylvania Poetry Society) and *Challenges for the Delusional.* Her collection, *Our Place in Line,* won Tiger's Eye Press' 2015 Chapbook Competition. Retired, she lives in Pennsylvania and rarely munches on donuts.

Jim Daniels' fifteenth book of poems, *Rowing Inland,* was published by Wayne State University Press. He has also published five collections of fiction and written four produced screenplays. He is the Baker University Professor of English at Carnegie Mellon University. After his first communion, he ate donuts on the ping-pong table in his parents' basement, which was his second communion.

Heather Lynne Davis is the author of *The Lost Tribe of Us,* her first book which won the Main Street Rag Poetry Book Award. Her poems have appeared in *Cream City Review, Poet Lore, Puerto del Sol,* and elsewhere She is Publications Manager for the Spring project and appreciates the hard lessons learned working in a donut shop.

Joanie DiMartino is the author of two collections of poetry, *Licking the Spoon* and *Strange Girls*. Her work has been published in such journals as *Modern Haiku, Alimentum,* and *Calyx*. A past winner of the Betty Gabehart Award for Poetry, she is a history museum director and consultant in Connecticut.

Lynn Domina is the author of two collections of poetry, *Corporal Works* and *Framed in Silence*, and the editor of a collection of essays, *Poets on the Psalms*. Her work appears in *New Letters, Nimrod, The Gettysburg Review*, and elsewhere. She lives in Michigan and serves as Head of the English Department at Northern Michigan University.

Denise Duhamel is the author of numerous collections of poetry, most recently *Scald* (Pittsburgh, 2017). *Blowout* (Pittsburgh, 2013) was a finalist for the National Book Critics Circle Award. She is a recipient of fellowships from the Guggenhiem Foundation and the NEA, and her work has appeared in eight editions of *The Best American Poetry* series. She is a professor at Florida International University in Miami.

Jane Ebihara is the author of a chapbook, *A Little Piece of Mourning* (Finishing Line Press, 2014). Her poems have been anthologized in *The Doll Collection* and *A Final Lilt of Songs* and published in such journals as *Tiferet, Adanna Literary Journal,* and *U.S. 1 Worksheets*. She is a retired teacher living in New Jersey.

Sara Eddy teaches writing at Smith College in Northampton, Massachusetts. Her poems have appeared in *Surreal Poetics* and *Panoply*. Donuts are her salvation and her nemesis.

Cal Freeman is the author of *Fight Songs* (Eyewear Publishing), *Brother of Leaving* (Marick Press), and the chapbook *Heard Among the Windbreak* (Eyewear). His writing has appeared in many journals, including *Passages North, The Cortland Review,* and *Hippocampus*. He teaches at Oakland University and lives in Michigan.

Anne Graue is the author of *Fig Tree in Winter* (Dancing Girl Press, 2017). Her work has appeared in numerous journals including the *Westchester Review,* the *Plath Poetry Project,* and the *Margaret Atwood Society Journal*. She is a writing instructor as well as a reviewer for *NewPages*. She lives in New York.

Justin Hamm is the author of *American Ephemeral* and *Lessons in Ruin,* as well as two poetry chapbooks. His work has appeared in *Nimrod, The Midwest Quarterly, Sugar House Review,* and elsewhere, and has been selected for *New Poetry from the Midwest* (New American Press, 2014) and the Stanley Hanks Memorial Poetry Prize from the St. Louis Poetry Center. He lives near Twain territory in Missouri.

Penny Harter's collections include *The Resonance Around Us, One Bowl,* and *Recycling Starlight.* She has won three fellowships from the NJ State Council on the Arts as well as the Mary Carolyn Davies Award from the PSA. She lives in New Jersey and offers writing workshops through Stockton University. She often stops for coffee and her favorite donut, a sugared twist, on her way to meetings.

David Hernandez's most recent poetry collection is *Dear, Sincerely* (University of Pittsburgh Press, 2016). He has been awarded an NEA Literature Fellowship, two Pushcart Prizes, and the Kathryn A. Morton Prize in Poetry. He teaches creative writing at California State University, Long Beach. A stack of pink boxes filled with donuts is his favorite minimalist sculpture.

Tina Kelley's third poetry collection, *Abloom and Awry,* was published by CavanKerry Press, joining *Precise* and *The Gospel of Galore,* winner of a 2003 Washington State Book Award. She co-authored *Almost Home: Helping Kids Move from Homelessness to Hope,* and reported for *The New York Times* for ten years, sharing in a staff Pulitzer for 9/11 coverage. She won the 2017 Jacar Press Chapbook Competition.

Kim Lozano teaches creative writing for the St. Louis Writers Workshop and St. Louis Oasis, a lifelong learning organization for people over 50. Her essays, poetry, and short fiction have appeared in *Poetry Daily, The Iowa Review, Alaska Quarterly Review,* and elsewhere. Although she'll take a donut shop donut to commercially packaged any day, she thinks the word "Hostess" is a beautiful word.

Marjorie Maddox has published eleven collections of poetry, including *True, False, None of the Above* (Poiema Poetry Series), an Illumination Book Award medalist. She is also the author of a short story collection, *What She Was Saying* (Fomite Press). She is a Professor of English and Creative Writing at Lock Haven University in Pennsylvania. Her favorite donut is the Boston cream.

Charlotte Mandel is the author of ten books of poetry, most recently *To Be the Daylight* (White Violet Press). Previous titles include *Through a Garden Gate* and two poem-novellas of feminist biblical revision—*The Life of Mary* and *The Marriages of Jacob*. Her awards include the New Jersey Poets Prize and two fellowships in poetry from the New Jersey State Council on the Arts.

Faisal Mohyuddin teaches English at Highland Park High School in Illinois and is a recent fellow in the U.S. Department of State's Teachers for Global Classrooms program. His poems have appeared in *Narrative, Crab Orchard Review, Rhino,* and elsewhere. He received the 2014 Edward Stanley Award from *Prairie Schooner.* When it comes to donuts, he prefers them old-fashioned.

Matthew Murrey's poems have appeared in journals such as *Tar River Poetry, Rhino,* and *Rattle.* He is the recipient of an NEA Fellowship in Poetry. A high school librarian, he lives in Illinois. He has eaten more donuts than he has done, but doing them is sweeter.

Richard Newman is the author of three poetry collections, most recently *All the Wasted Beauty of the World* (Able Muse Press, 2014.) He is also the author of the novel *Graveyard of the Gods* (Bank Slate Press, 2016). His poetry and prose have appeared in *Best American Poetry, Boulevard, Crab Orchard Review,* and elsewhere. He currently lives on Majuro, an atoll in the Marshall Islands.

Michael Northen edits *Wordgathering, A Journal of Disability and Poetry* and is co-editor of the anthology, *Beauty Is a Verb: The New Poetry of Disability,* and the disability short fiction anthology, *The Right Way to Be Crippled and Naked.* An educator for more than forty years, he has taught adults with disabilities, women on public assistance, prisoners, and rural and inner city children. He lives in NJ.

Elizabeth O'Brien is the author of a chapbook, *A Secret History of World Wide Outage* (Diode Editions, 2018). She is the recipient of a Minnesota Emerging Writers' Grant through the Loft Literary Center and the James Wright Poetry Award from the Academy of American Poets. Her work has appeared in such journals as *New England Review, The Rumpus,* and *Ploughshares.* She currently lives in Minnesota.

Keli Osborn's poems appear in the chapbook, *How to Love Everything,* and the anthologies, *The Absence of Something Specified* and *All We Can Hold.* Her writing also appears in the *San Pedro River Review* and *Elohi Gadugi*. She won the 2016 Pacific Northwest Poetry Contest from *Timberline Review* and Ooligan Press. A former manager in local government, she works with community organizations in Oregon. Her favorite donuts involve cream filling.

Martin Ott is the author of seven books of poetry and fiction, including *Underdays* (University of Notre Dame Press, 2015), which won the Sandeen Prize, and *Spectrum* (C&R Press, 2016). His work has appeared in such journals as *Harvard Review, North American Review,* and *Prairie Schooner.* A longtime resident of Los Angeles, his favorite donut is the old-fashioned.

Brent Pallas lives and works in New York City as a freelance designer of craft and home projects. His poetry has appeared in *The Missouri Review, Poetry, The Southern Review,* and elsewhere. He favors cream-filled strawberry donuts with sprinkles and is having one right now with a cup of coffee while reading this anthology.

A native New Yorker, **James Penha** has lived for the past quarter-century in Indonesia. He was a finalist for the 2017 Saints and Sinners Short Fiction Contest and an essay of his was featured in *The New York Times'* "Modern Love" column in 2016. He edits *New Verse News*, an online journal of current events poetry.

Anjela Villarreal Ratliff is a retired elementary school teacher who is now a creative writing workshop presenter. Her poems have appeared in various publications, including *The Crafty Poet II: A Portable Workshop, Pilgrimage,* and *Bearing the Mask: Southwestern Persona Poems*. She lives in Texas.

Meg Reynolds' poems have appeared in such publications as *The Missing Slate, Mid-American Review*, and the anthology, *Monster Verse: Poems Human and Inhuman*. She is the co-director of writinginsideVT, an organization that offers writing instruction at the Chittenden Regional Correctional Facility. She lives and teaches in Vermont.

Mira Rosenthal is the author of *The Local World,* recipient of the Wick Poetry Prize. Her second book of translations, *Colonies,* won the Northern California Book Award. She is a past fellow of the NEA and Stanford University's Stegner Program. Her work has appeared in such journals as *Ploughshares, Threepenny Review,* and *Harvard Review*. She teaches in Cal Poly's creative writing program.

Marybeth Rua-Larsen is the author of the chapbook *Nothing In-Between* (Barefoot Muse Press). Her poems have appeared in *Cleaver, Measure, American Arts Quarterly*, and elsewhere. She won the 2016 Parent-Writer Fellowship in Poetry from the Martha's Vineyard Institute of Creative Writing and the 2017 Luso-American Fellowship for the Disquiet International Literary Program in Lisbon, Portugal. She teaches at Bristol Community College in Massachusetts.

Anne Sandor earned a BA from Vassar College and an MFA in Creative Writing from Vermont College. She is an Associate Professor of English and Writing Consultancy Coordinator at SUNY Orange in Middletown, NY, where she teaches Contemporary Novel and Creative Writing. After years working with students on their fiction, she now works on her own stories and poems. A Brooklyn native, she still believes it's Leske's for the best jelly doughnuts.

Martha Silano is the author of four books of poetry, most recently *Reckless Lovely* and *The Little Office of the Immaculate Conception*, winner of the 2010 Saturnalia Books Poetry Prize. She also co-edited *The Daily Poet: Day-By-Day Prompts for Your Writing Practice*. Her poems have appeared in such journals as *Poetry, Paris Review,* and *New England Review*. She teaches at Bellevue College and lives in Washington State.

Julian Stannard is a Reader in English and Creative Writing at the University of Winchester (UK); he runs the MA in Creative Writing program, which attracts students from across the world. His most recent collection is *What were you thinking?* (CB Editions, London, 2016), and his work appears in *Poetry, Salamander, Manhattan Review,* and elsewhere.

Carole Stone is the author of four poetry collections, most recently *Late* (Turning Point, 2016). Her poems have been published in *Slab, Cavewall, Bellevue Literary Review,* and elsewhere. She is Distinguished Professor Emerita of English and creative writing at Montclair State University. She divides her time between Springs, East Hampton, and Verona, New Jersey.

Tim Suermondt is the author of five full-length collections of poetry, including *The World Doesn't Know You* (Pinyon Publishing, 2017) and *Josephine Baker Swimming Pool* (MadHat Press). His poems have appeared in *Poetry, The Georgia Review, Ploughshares,* and elsewhere. He lives in Cambridge, Massachusetts, and favors chocolate donuts.

Katrin Talbot is the author of four chapbooks, most recently *The Little Red Poem* from dancing girl press. A song cycle based on her poetry was premiered in Toronto. Australian-born, she now lives in Wisconsin, where she is a photographer, makes viola noise, and writes. She once received enough prize money from a national poetry contest to fund a donut run.

Marilyn L. Taylor, former Poet Laureate of Wisconsin, is the author of eight poetry collections. Her work has appeared in *Poetry, Mezzo Cammin, Rhino,* and elsewhere. She won the Margaret Reid prize for formal verse in 2015. She taught poetry for fifteen years at the University of Wisconsin-Milwaukee, and has never confronted a donut she didn't like.

Eileen Van Hook's poetry has appeared in such journals as *U.S. 1 Work Sheets, Paterson Literary Review,* and *Gravel.* She placed first in a poetry contest in *Writer's Journal* and won second place in the 2017 Allen Ginsberg Poetry Contest. She is a retired municipal clerk now living and writing in the wilds of northwestern New Jersey.

Dianalee Velie is the author of five books of poetry, most recently *Ever After.* She is the founder of the John Hay Poetry Society and is a member of the Vermont Branch of the National League of American Pen Women, the New England Poetry Club, the International Woman Writers Guild, and the New Hampshire Poetry Society. She is the Poet Laureate of Newbury, New Hampshire.

Charles Harper Webb's latest book, *Brain Camp,* was published in 2015 by the University of Pittsburgh Press. *A Million MFAs Are Not Enough,* a collection of essays on contemporary American poetry, was published by Red Hen Press in 2016. Recipient of grants from the Whiting and Guggenheim foundations, he teaches creative writing at California State University, Long Beach.

Anne Harding Woodworth is the author of five books of poetry, most recently *Unattached Male.* An excerpt from one of her four chapbooks, *The Last Gun,* won the 2016 COG Poetry Prize. Her work appears in journals in the U.S. and abroad. Her career was with the Chrysler Corporation, and her favorite donuts involve cars. She is co-chair of the Poetry Board at the Folger Shakespeare Library, Washington, DC.

Credits

About the Editors

Jason Lee Brown is a freelance writer and editor from central Illinois. He earned an MFA in Creative Writing from Southern Illinois University Carbondale. He is the author of a historical novel, *Prowler: The Mad Gasser of Mattoon*, as well as a novella, *Championship Run*, and a poetry chapbook, *Blue Collar Fathers*.

Shanie Latham earned an MFA in Creative Writing from Southern Illinois University Carbondale. Her work has appeared in *Big Muddy*, *Boulevard*, and *Slant*. She is an editor at *River Styx*, series co-editor of *New Stories from the Midwest*, and an associate professor of English at Jefferson College in Missouri.

CPSIA information can be obtained
at www.ICGtesting.com
Printed in the USA
BVHW03s0747051018
529147BV00052B/802/P